I Wonder What My Marine Is Doing Now

A Day in the Life of a Deployed United States Marine

Written by Fritz Stokes

Illustrated by Courtney Jones

Digital Enhancements by Kaitlin Stokes

Published by:

Little Oaks

Little Oaks Publishing
18896 Greenwell Springs Road
Greenwell Springs, LA 70739
www.thepublishedword.com

ISBN: 978-1-950398-13-3

Printed on demand
For Worldwide Distribution

The heart and soul behind this book involves the sacrifice all military families endure while serving across the globe. They know first-hand that "Freedom Isn't Free."

A small tent

A big tent

Metal buildings called "hooches"

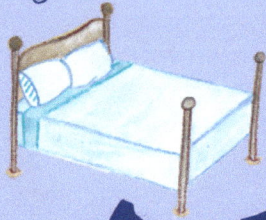

A sleeping area in a forward operating base

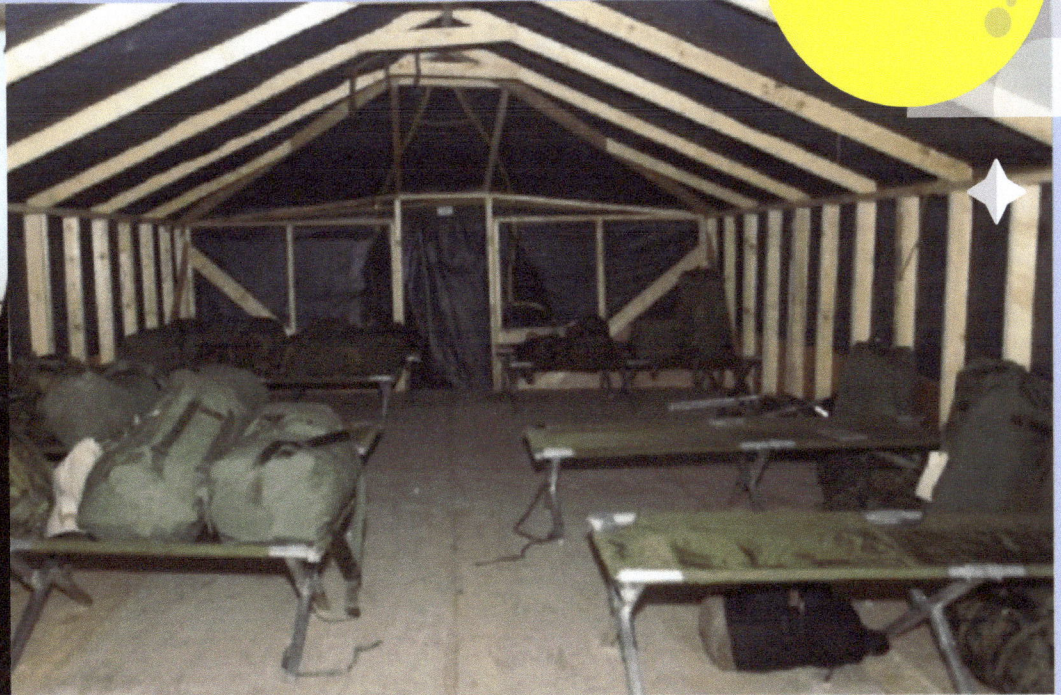
Cots inside a large, wood-framed tent

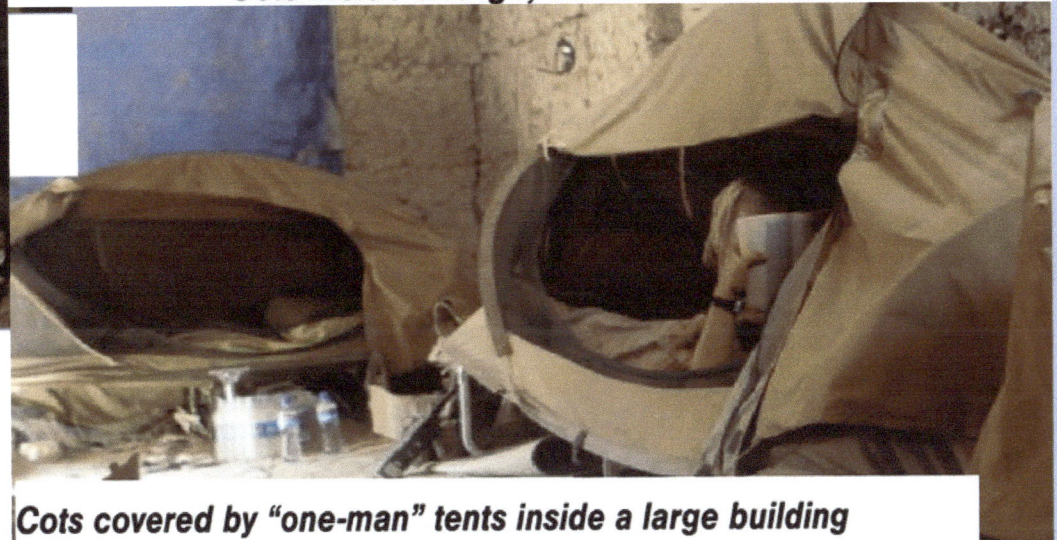
Cots covered by "one-man" tents inside a large building

I wonder where Marines eat when they're deployed.

They could be eating in a "field chowhall," but sometimes they may be eating outside, like when you're at a picnic.

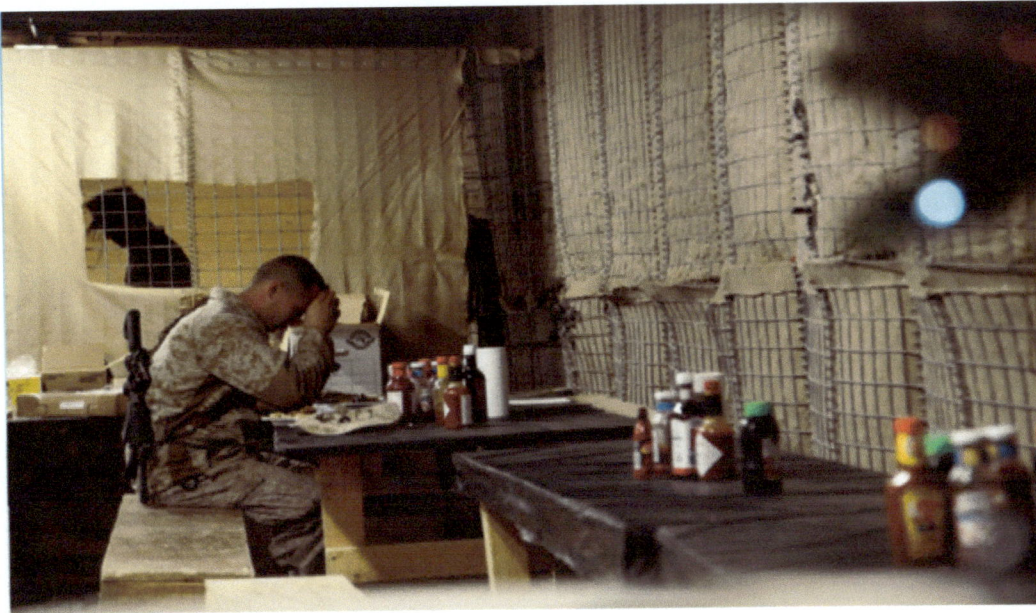

Praying before a meal in a field chow hall

Serving food in a field chow hall

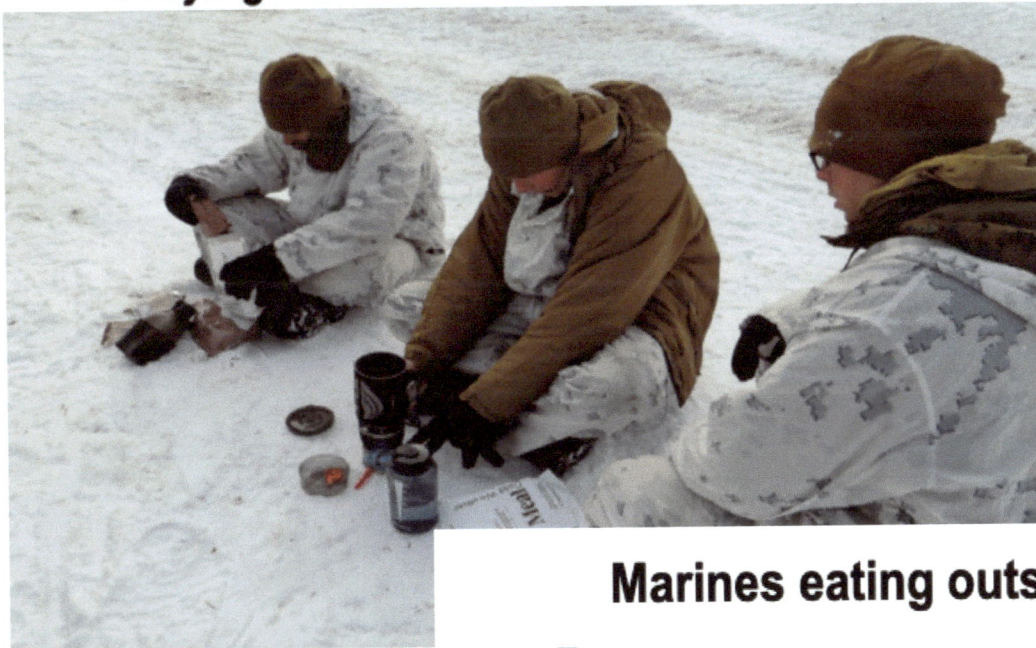

Marines eating outside like a picnic

I wonder what Marines eat when they're deployed.

If they're eating in a chow hall, they will be eating the same meals they ate with you at home. If they are eating outside, they will be eating a type of take-out food called Meals Ready to Eat (MREs).

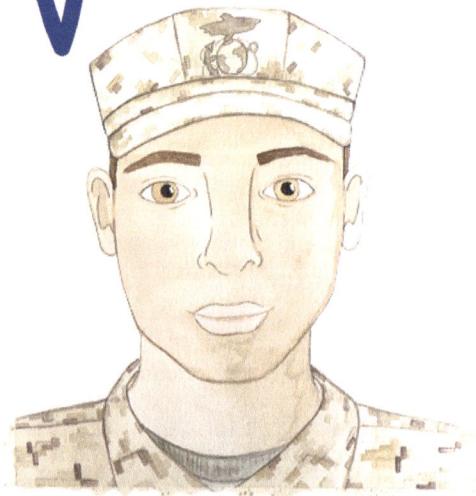

Meal Ready to Eat "MRE"

Crumb cake served in a Field Chow Hall

Hot meals are always good to have

I wonder what kind of bathrooms Marines have.

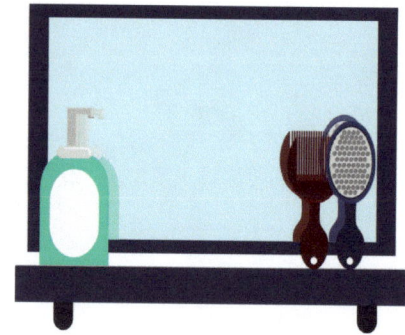

Marines use "Port-a-Potties" just like the kind you see at soccer fields or other outdoor places.

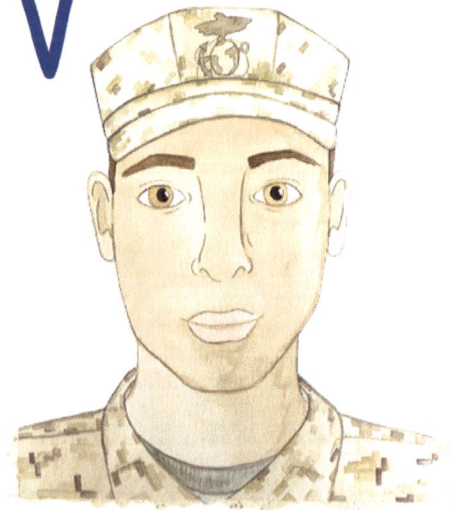

I wonder where Marines get water to drink and wash with.

Marines pump water from lakes, rivers, or the ocean and put it into a special machine that makes the water clean and safe to use. This clean water is then stored in "Water Bulls" and moved to areas where the Marines can have access to it.

A Marine pumping water from a river

A water bull

Marines using a special machine to clean the water so it's safe to drink

I wonder how Marines brush their teeth and wash up.

Marines living in big base camps use sinks inside a large tent. Marines staying out "in the field" at Patrol Bases brush their teeth and wash up using a water bottle.

I wonder how Marines take a shower.

Marines living in a base camp use a shower inside a shower tent. If they live in a smaller camp, they may use a bucket-shower, which is a plastic bucket with small holes in the bottom so that water slowly drains out.

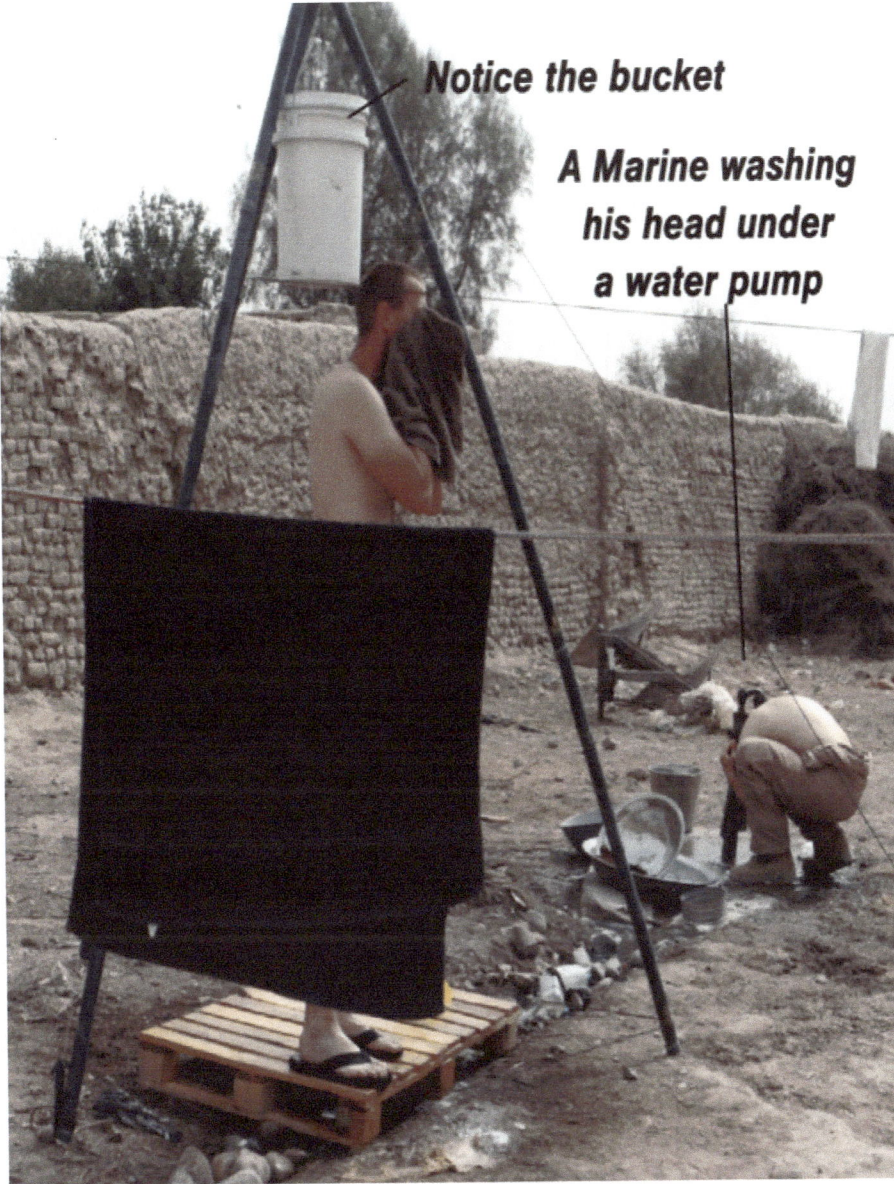

Notice the bucket

A Marine washing his head under a water pump

Front door of a shower unit

Homemade shower

A field shower unit used at larger base camps

I wonder how Marines wash their clothes.

Marines living in a big base camp can wash their clothes in a big washing machine, just like they do at home. If they are living outside (like camping), they probably use a small bucket to wash their clothes.

Washing machines inside a tent

I wonder what Marines do when they aren't working.

Marines living in a big base camp have access to the Internet and can play video games, watch TV, read a book, play sports or lift weights to stay in shape.

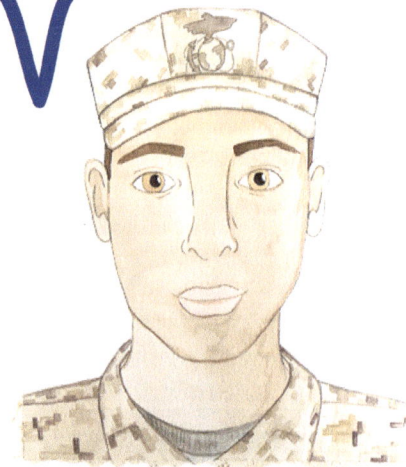

A volleyball game between Marines and Afghan police

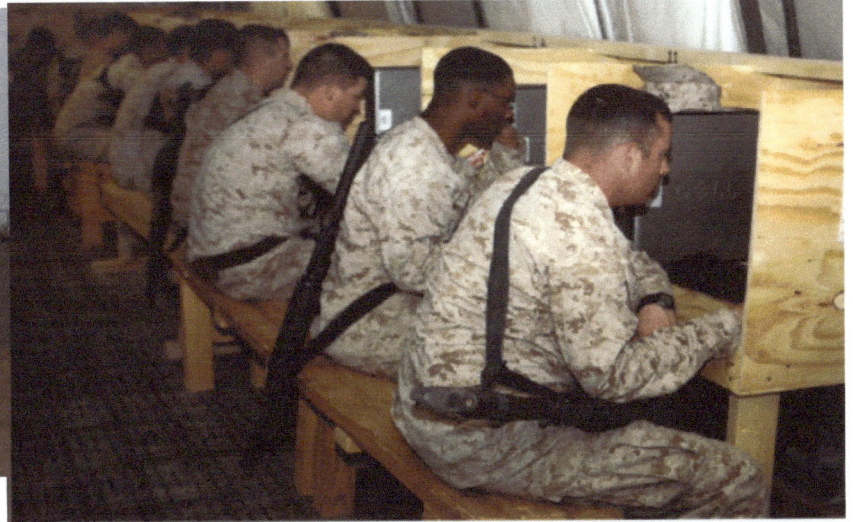

Computer booths at a base camp

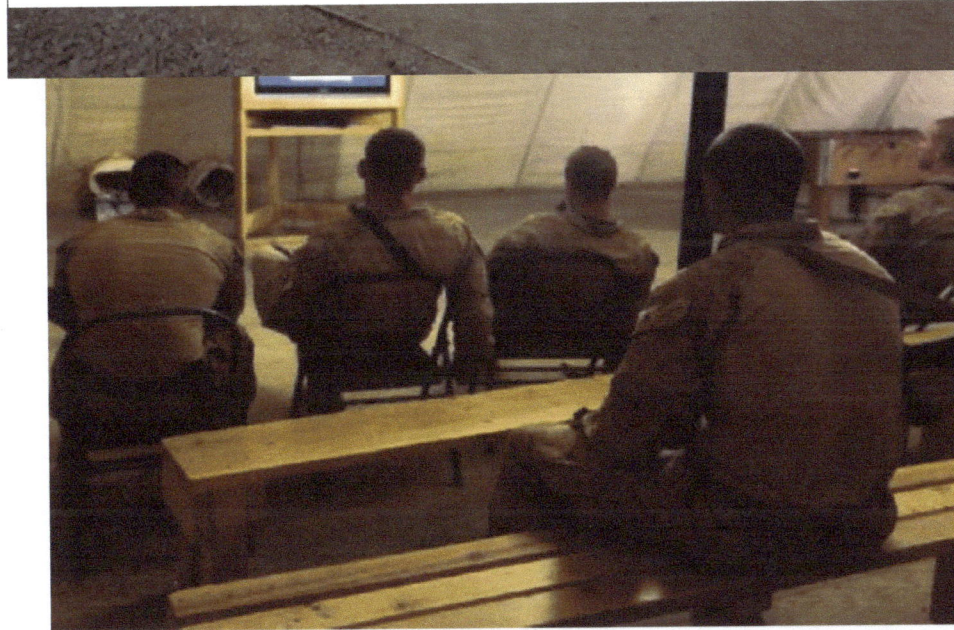

Watching TV in a recreation tent at a base camp

Capt. Emma Woods takes 1st in the Crossfit Challenge

I wonder how my Marine will get back to me.

Your Marine will probably come home with a group of other Marines on a bus or airplane. There will be lots of other families waiting to welcome back their Marine.

I wonder when my Marine will get back to me.

Your Marine is counting down the days too and can't wait to get back home and give you a hug! For now, you need to know your Marine is doing all of the same things they would do with you. And, no matter where your Marine is right now, that includes loving you very much!

The author, who at the time was SSgt. Fritz Stokes, USMC, coming home to his family after deploying to Desert Storm/Desert Shield for six and a half months. Pictured with him is his 5-year-old son, Andrew

Dedication and Acknowledgments

First and foremost, I thank Almighty God for His love, mercy and grace given through His loving Son, Jesus Christ.

This book is also dedicated to my devoted wife and best friend , Kathryn, who stood by my side during all the deployments and PCS moves we went through during our time of service in the United States Marine Corps.

A special thanks goes to my grown children—Andrew, Niki and Kaitlin—for their encouragement during this project.

I also wish to thank my good friends, Bill and Vivian Joseph (who both served in the Marine Corps), as well as Rylan and Sloane Stouffer (who carried on during their father's numerous deployments) for their insightful suggestions and help.

A very special thank you is also given to Col. and Mrs. Krockel for allowing their amazing daughter, Sophia, to appear on the cover. Sophia represents well all the dedicated military families this book is meant for.

Finally, a note of encouragement to my fellow classroom teachers, counselors and other school personnel directly supporting the children of our brave military men and women. May this book be a valuable tool that enables the precious children you work with to gain a sense of peace and a feeling of connection, knowing that in the midst of separation from their special U.S. Marine, he or she is still going about his or her usual day-to-day routines and will pick right back up on those same routines upon returning to his or her family's waiting arms.

— *Fritz Stokes*

To my parents and family, who have always supported and encouraged my creative endeavors.

To the Lord, for blessings, opportunities and ability.

To all my Marine Corps friends, thank you for doing life with me and letting me share in yours.

To my amazing students, thank you for all of the hugs and smiles, and for making my days more colorful!

— *Courtney Jones*

Photograph Credits

www.ingramcontent.com/pod-product-compliance
Lightning Source LLC
Chambersburg PA
CBHW040453100426

42813CB00021BA/2986